Recipes for Gourmet Vegetables
by Glenn Andrews

Introduction

Daikon, tomatillos, bok choy, arugula, radicchio. Suddenly, these and other gourmet vegetables are turning up in produce departments and seed catalogs across the country. But what are they, and how do you use them?

Even those who are adventurous in the kitchen are reluctant to buy something they have no idea what to do with. These vegetables are unusual to us just because we're not used to them yet. In their home countries, they're in everyday use. Don't pass them by because of lack of knowledge about them. They're delicious! And I, for one, an delighted to be living at a time in which they've become available. We've come a long way from the days, not so long ago, when even canned water chestnuts were hard to find.

This bulletin can be your guide to the most interesting of the new-to-the-market vegetables. They're listed alphabetically, with a description of each and suggestions for use plus recipes. The alphabetization is by the main part of the name, not necessarily its first word. Thus, Japanese eggplant can be found under E, for eggplant, etc.

Most of the vegetables can easily be grown from seed. A list of sources appears at the back of the bulletin. Often, the name used by supermarkets is different from that given in seed catalogs. Thus, you'll usually find *bok choy* in your produce department, but *pak choi* is the seed to buy. Alternate names are included wherever this applies.

Try these recipes and suggestions to familiarize yourself with the ingredients, then create your own ways to use them. You can combine recipes, using the cooking method from one and the flavoring from another. You can use whatever herbs or spices strike your fancy, experiment with different liquids--and in general, have fun!

Jerusalem Artichokes

The Jerusalem artichoke is a little gem of a root vegetable which can be eaten raw, when it resembles water chestnuts, or cooked, when it resembles nothing but its own marvelous self. It's often called *sunchoke* in markets.

Fry as you would potato chips. Or peel, boil and serve creamed. I have read that if boiled much beyond the point of tenderness, they will again become tough.

Growing Jerusalem artichokes is almost ridiculously easy. You can use special seed tubers or simply plant *sunchokes* from a supermarket. Use small tubers whole; cut bigger ones into two or more pieces, each containing an eye. Plant in early spring, six inches deep, one foot apart, in full sun. You'll get a towering plant (up to ten feet high) and small flowers which resemble sunflowers. In late fall, dig up your surprisingly large crop. From six medium-sized tubers, I once got 20 pounds of sunchokes. Choose a spot where you won't mind having a permanent *sunchoke* patch, since unless you dig up every single last tuber, they'll come back year after year.

Purée of Jerusalem Artichokes

This is a fantastically good dish, and a fine introduction to the joys of the sunchoke.

1 pound Jerusalem artichokes (*sunchokes*)
6 tablespoons butter
6 tableapoons heavy cream
salt and freshly ground black pepper to taste

Peel the Jerusalem artichokes, then cut them into chunks. Boil in water to cover for 10 to 15 minutes or until very tender. Drain, then run the chunks in a food processor along with the butter and heavy cream until smooth. Reheat gently, stirring and seasoning to taste with the salt and pepper. Serves 4.

Arugula

No one paid much attention to *arugula* (pronounced uh-roo-gulla) when it was called *roquette* or *rocket*. Now that the marketers have reverted to the Italian name, cooks have discovered its nutlike taste, and it's become a very trendy food. Use it raw in salads and sandwiches or chopped and cooked in purées, soups, souffles and sauces for pasta.

Easily grown from seed (sometimes under the name *rugula*); given the same care as any loose-leaf lettuce, it will be ready for use in 35 days.

Arugula-Pecan Sauce for Pasta

3 tablespoons olive oil
2 tablespoons butter
1 bunch (2 cups) *arugula*, chopped
3 scallions, minced
1/4 cup pecan halves
10 cherry tomatoes, cut in half
1/2 cup freshly grated Parmesan cheese
2 cups light cream
salt and freshly ground black pepper

Heat the olive oil and butter in a large frying pan over medium heat. Add the *arugula*, scallions and pecans and cook, stirring, for three or four minutes. Add the tomatoes, cheese and cream. Simmer, stirring gently and often, until a little thicker then heavy cream. Season to taste. Makes enough sauce for 1 pound of pasta.

Fresh Bean Sprouts

Most supermarkets have carried fresh bean sprouts (the sprouts of mung beans) for several years now, but most of their customers still don't know what to do with them. Once you've tried them, you'll never again buy the canned variety. Use the fresh ones whenever bean sprouts are called for in recipes--or sprinkle them on salads--or cook them in such excellent, quick-cooking vegetable dishes as either version of Bean Sprouts with Peppers, below. You can substitute other vegetables for the peppers with equally happy results--chopped celery and/or tomatoes, for instance, go well with sprouts, as do onions.

It's easy to grow your own bean sprouts. First buy mung beans, which you can find at most health food stores and many supermarkets. It's possible to buy special sprouting apparatus, but a 1-quart jar is really all you need. Put 1/2 cup of the mung beans in the jar and add about 2 cups of warm water. Cover loosely. The next day, drain the beans in a colander and rinse them gently with warm water. Drain again, return to the jar. Cover loosely and put it in a cupboard or other dark place. Repeat the rinsing and draining process every day for three or four days until the sprouts are about one inch long. They can be eaten right away or stored, refrigerated, for five or six days.

American Sautéed Bean Sprouts and Peppers

This is a quick and delicious vegetable dish, the kind you can cook without even thinking about what you're doing.

2 tablespoons butter
2 cups fresh bean sprouts
2 sweet peppers--green, red, yellow, orange, purple or
    whatever--deseeded and diced
salt and freshly ground black pepper to taste

Melt the butter in a frying pan over medium heat, then add the bean sprouts and peppers and sauté, stirring, for 3 or 4 minutes. Season to taste. Serves 3 to 4.

Chinese Bean Sprouts and Peppers

This version takes more thought and a bit more time to prepare, but when you eat it, you'll think you're in a four-star Chinese restaurant.

2 tablespoons oil
2 sweet peppers, halved, deseeded and thinly sliced
1/2 teaspoon finely minced or pressed garlic
1 teaspoon finely minced fresh ginger
1/2 teaspoon salt
2 cups fresh bean sprouts
1/4 cup water
1 teaspoon sherry
1/4 teaspoon sugar
Oriental hot oil to taste

Heat the oil over medium-high heat in a wok or large frying pan. Stir-fry the peppers, garlic, ginger and salt for about one minute. Add the bean sprouts and stir-fry for another minute. Add the water. Cover and cook for 2 minutes. Stir in the sherry and sugar, then the hot oil--start with 2 or 3 drops, then add more, drop by drop, till the dish is as hot as you wish. Serves 3 to 4.

Bok Choy

Bok choy is the variety of cabbage most used in Chinese cooking. It can be spotted by its thick white stalks and dark green leaves. You can use it as you would any other cabbage (it makes a wonderful cole slaw), or use it in traditional Far Eastern recipes.

Baby *bok choy* (about 5 or 6 inches long) is choice, though hard to find. The best way to get it is to grow your own. Most seed companies carry *bok choy* seed, though usually under the name *pak choi*. It will mature in 45 days, but baby *bok choy* will be ready somewhat earlier than that.

Sweet and Sour Bok Choy

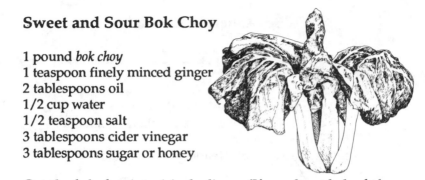

1 pound *bok choy*
1 teaspoon finely minced ginger
2 tablespoons oil
1/2 cup water
1/2 teaspoon salt
3 tablespoons cider vinegar
3 tablespoons sugar or honey

Cut the *bok choy* into 1-inch slices. (If you have baby *bok choy*, just cut it in two lengthwise.) Heat the oil in a wok or large frying pan over medium-high heat, then add the *bok choy* and ginger and stir-fry for 1 minute. Turn the heat down to medium, stir in the water and salt, cover, cook for 3 minutes. Add the vinegar and the sugar or honey, then stir over fairly high heat until the sauce has thickened. Serves 3 to 4.

Celeriac

Celeriac (also known as celery root) isn't going to win any beauty contests. It's knobby and usually a bit mottled looking. Those knobs and mottlings, though, hide a vegetable with a mild celery taste and a nice, firm texture.

Peel it, then par-boil briefly to tame down the flavor. Use it in salads, stews or soups or simply diced and boiled, then buttered and seasoned with rosemary or sage.

Although the common name for celeriac is celery root, it's not the same plant. Grow it as you would any other root vegetable. Seeds are widely available, sometimes under the French name, *celeri-rave*.

Celeri Remoulade

A classic French first course, Celeri Remoulade also makes a fine salad.

1/2 pound celeriac, peeled and cut into matchsticks
1/2 cup real mayonnaise (preferably homemade)
1 tablespoon Dijon mustard
chopped fresh herbs (parsley, for instance)

Blanch the celeriac by plunging in boiling water for 1 minute. Drain and cool, then combine with the mayonnaise and mustard. Chill well. Serve on lettuce leaves. Sprinkle the fresh herbs on top. Serves 3 to 4.

Purée of Celeriac and Potato Soup

Move over, vichyssoise. This soup's much better, hot or cold.

1/2 pound celeriac, peeled and thinly sliced
2 medium-sized potatoes, peeled and sliced
1/4 teaspoon minced garlic
1 medium onion, minced
3 tablespoons butter or margarine
4 cups chicken broth
salt and pepper to taste
(plus cream and minced chives if you're serving it cold)

Boil the celeriac in water for 5 minutes. Drain, then put into a medium-sized saucepan with the potatoes, garlic, onion and butter. Cook over medium-low heat, stirring, for 5 minutes. Add the chicken broth and simmer, covered, until everything is tender (about 20 minutes). Purée in a food processor or blender or put through a food mill. Season with salt and pepper.

To serve cold, cool a bit, then add light cream to thin the purée down to a vichyssoise-like consistency. Chill well. Serve topped with chives. Serves 4 to 6.

Chayotes

Chayotes (pronounced chy-<u>oh</u>-tay) are fun. They look a bit like pears which went slightly wrong--darkish green, with deep lengthwise ridges and very large, edible seeds. In taste and texture, they're rather like a cross between summer and winter squashes.

Cook *chayotes* as you would zucchini or any other summer squash or boil them, whole, for half and hour, then split, stuff and bake at 350° F. for 15 minutes as you might winter squash.

For those who live in a warm climate, *chayotes* are easy to grow. Use supermarket- bought *chayotes*, either the seeds or the entire vegetable. Plant about 1 inch deep in a sunny spot in the spring. You'll almost immediately have luxuriant vines with large, pretty leaves. (Give them something to grow on or they will take off over trees and rooftops.) In the fall they will produce tiny flowers which soon become *chayotes*.

Steamed, Buttered Chayotes

This is the way I first tasted *chayotes*, and the way I still like best. I saw this strange-looking vegetable in a market, bought some, took them home and just plain cooked them.

2 large *chayotes*, peeled and diced (dice and cook
    the huge seed, too)
2 tablespoons butter
salt and freshly ground black pepper to taste

Steam or boil the diced *chayotes* for 10 to 15 minutes or until very tender. Drain if necessary, then combine with the butter and season to taste. Serves 3 to 4.

Chilies

What *are* all those different chilies, some fresh, some dried, you can find in supermarkets these days? Which ones are searingly hot, which are not? They're very confusing, and the situation is not helped by the fact that regional names have recently been given to some of them. (What, for instance, is the 'New Mexico' chili you can suddenly see in produce departments?) It would take a whole bulletin to explain them all, so we'll just tackle a few of the more usable ones here. For a fuller explanation, see one of Diana Kennedy's definitive Mexican cookbooks.

A useful (though not infallible) rule of thumb is that the smaller the chili, the hotter it is. Thus the *serrano* chili, which is the size of a little finger, can take the top of your head off, and the *jalapeno*, a little larger but still small, is almost as efficient at this task. *Poblanos*, quite large, are mild (though an occasional one can set you on fire).

Heat isn't everything, though. Each sort of chili has its own flavor. In fact, most authoritative Mexican cooks claim that the point of a chili is the flavor, not the heat. *Pasilla* chilies add a pleasant richness; *jalapenos*--well, you know what they taste like, since they're the chilies used in nachos.

To prepare fresh chilies: 'Roast' either under a broiler or by holding them directly in a flame until the skin blackens in spots and is well blistered. Put into a plastic bag and allow to 'sweat' for 15 minutes. Peel; cut a slit, remove seeds and veins.

To prepare dried chilies: This can vary depending on how you plan to use the chilies, but in general: 'Toast' by turning them on a hot griddle for a few minutes. When cool, remove the seeds and veins, soak what's left in cool water for 30 minutes.

Always wear rubber gloves when working with chilies, and keep your hands away from your face and especially your eyes.

Fresh chilies are simple to grow from seed. Treat them as you would any sweet pepper. Seeds are available from most catalogs (see p. 32). Park Seed Company carries nine varieties.

Frances Thompson's Mixed Dried Chilies

If you keep a little bag of this mixture on hand, you'll find it a real boon for jazzing up pasta, soups, stews, scrambled eggs and various bland dishes. Sprinkle in a little or a lot (a lot would be about one teaspoon per person), depending on your tolerance for heat.

Gather up a handful of each of two or three of the bewildering array of dried chilies you'll find at many supermarkets--'New Mexico' chilies, for instance, and *pasillas*. Remove the seeds if you want a milder mixture. Run the chilies together in a food processor or blender until they're fairly finely chopped but not approaching a powder. Store at room temperature, tightly closed.

Chilies Rellenos con Queso

6 *poblana* (or 'California') chilies, roasted, seeded and
    peeled (see Chilies, p. 10)
1/2 pound Monterey Jack or Cheddar cheese, cut into 6 strips
flour
3 eggs, separated
oil for frying
tomato sauce (optional--see below)

Stuff the chilies with the cheese. Dry well with paper towels, then coat with flour. Heat about 1 inch of oil in a wok or large frying pan over fairly high heat. Beat the egg whites and yolks separately and thoroughly, then fold together. Coat each stuffed chile carefully with this batter and fry until puffed and light brown, turning frequently.

Serve now or make ahead, then reheat in a thin tomato sauce. (They'll re-puff.) One good sauce would be the *salsa* given under *tomatillos*, using regular red tomatoes instead of *tomatillos* and thinning it down with a little chicken broth or water and blending it until smooth. Serves 6.

Chinese Long Beans

Chinese long beans are very thin and about 12 to 14 inches long. They can be cut into appropriate lengths and cooked in a stir-fry or used in any recipe which calls for green beans. (Since long beans are a bit less tender, add a few minutes to the cooking time.) In Southern California, where Chinese long beans are widely available but small green beans are a rarity (large Kentucky Wonders are the norm there), many cooks use the Chinese variety for all their green bean cookery. The taste is slightly different, but the general effect is the same.

Chinese long beans (also called asparagus beans, or yard or yardlong beans) are easy to grow from seed. (Both Burpee's and Nichols carry them--see p. 32) They need trellises or strong stakes and are very prolific over a long season.

Stir-Fried Chinese Long Beans

This is a very basic recipe, designed to get you on speaking terms with the Chinese long bean. To it, you can add your choice of fresh ginger, sesame oil, hot oil, sherry, soy sauce and/or such Chinese condiments (available at most super- markets) as *hoisin* sauce, chili paste with garlic, etc.

3 tablespoons oil
1 pound Chinese long beans, trimmed and cut into
    1 1/2-inch lengths
1/2 teaspoon minced garlic
1/4 teaspoon salt
1/2 cup water
1/4 teaspoon sugar
2 grinds of black pepper from a mill

Heat oil in a wok or large frying pan over high heat. Add beans, garlic and salt. Stir-fry for about 10 seconds. Turn the heat down to medium, add the water, cover and cook for 5 minutes. Stir in sugar and pepper and serve at once. Serves 4.

Cilantro

Cilantro (pronounced see-<u>lahn</u>-tro) is fresh coriander, also known as Chinese parsley. It looks a lot like flat-leaved parsley, but has a very distinctive flavor. For me, it was hate at first bite, but now (thanks to a friend's serving the chicken salad below), I'm wild about it.

You'll find *cilantro* in other recipes in this bulletin--the Calypso Chicken under *plantains* and the salsa under *tomatillos*--but you can sprinkle it on any salad, cook it in any broth, soup or stew, or use it to top eggs or other dishes to which you want to add flavor and color. Any Mexican or Indian dish seems more authentic with the addition of a bit of it, too.

Cilantro is available all over the country these days and is also a cinch to grow. Seeds are readily available, usually under the name coriander, and you can even start some from the coriander seeds in your spice cabinet. You can get a dual harvest --*cilantro* greens and then the seeds, which have an entirely different taste.

Margaret Heath's Curried Chicken Salad

2 whole chicken breasts, simmered, skinned, boned and
    diced
2 stalks celery, destringed and diced
1/4 cup (or more if you've already learned to like it)
    chopped *cilantro*
1 cup mayonnaise
1 tablespoon finely minced onion
1 teaspoon curry powder (or more to taste)
lettuce leaves

Place the chicken, celery and *cilantro* in a bowl, then add a mixture of the mayonnaise, curry powder and onion. Serve on a bed of lettuce leaves, whole or shredded, and garnish with a little more *cilantro* sprinkled on top. Serves 4 as a main course.

Daikon

Daikon is the Japanese white radish, long and sometimes extremely big. Buy the smallest ones you can find since they have a better flavor. Cook them in stews and vegetable mixtures exactly as you would turnips, or slice, dice or cut into sticks and use with a dip or in a salad.

Daikon seed is available from many seed companies, sometimes under the names April Cross or Summer Cross. Culture is the same as for any radish, though *daikon* takes longer to mature.

Far Eastern Celery and Daikon Salad

1 pound *daikon*, peeled
2 ribs of celery, destringed
1/4 cup chopped parsley
1 tablespoon tamari or other dark soy sauce
1 tablespoon Oriental sesame oil
1/2 teaspoon honey
1 1/2 tablespoons rice vinegar

Cut *daikon* and celery into matchsticks about 2 inches long. Put them in a bowl, add the rest of the ingredients, toss well. Serve at room temperature. Serves 3 to 4.

Japanese Eggplant

Japanese eggplants are the tiny ones, thin and just a few inches long. They're sweet, creamy, small-seeded and tender-skinned. Because of their size, they are unsuitable for such traditional eggplant dishes as parmigiana or breaded slices, but they're a real treat when split lengthwise and sautéed or grilled.

If you look hard enough, you'll find the seed in most catalogs, though under a variety of such names as 'Tycoon.' Grow as you would any eggplant, but pick before they're any more than 5 inches long.

Oven-Roasted Japanese Eggplant

4 Japanese eggplants, caps removed
1 tablespoon olive oil
1/2 teaspoon salt

Split the eggplants in two lengthwise. Place them on a baking sheet, then sprinkle with olive oil and salt. Stir to coat them well, then bake, cut side down, at 375° F. for about 20 minutes, or until the down side is brown. Serves 2 to 4.

Glazed Japanese Eggplant Teriyaki

4 Japanese eggplants, caps removed
3 tablespoons salad or olive oil
1/4 cup teriyaki sauce (see p. 17)

Cut the eggplants in half, then into 1-inch slices. Brown them in the oil in a large frying pan over medium-high heat. Add the teriyaki sauce and continue to cook, stirring gently, until the eggplant pieces are nicely glazed. Serves 2 to 4.

Marinated, Broiled Japanese Eggplant

Actually, the eggplant is marinated twice, but it's still an easy preparation and terrific tasting.

6 Japanese eggplants, caps removed
3 tablespoons olive oil (divided)
1/4 teaspoon minced or pressed garlic
1 tablespoon Balsamic or red wine vinegar
1 tablespoon minced chives or fresh basil or a
    combination of the two
salt and freshly ground black pepper to taste

Split each eggplant lengthwise. Marinate for at least half an hour in garlic and 1 tablespoon of the oil. Broil, starting with the cut side toward the source of heat, for just a few minutes, until brown, turning twice. For the very best flavor, broil over charcoal.

Put on a plate or platter. Anoint with a mixture of the remaining 2 tablespoons of oil, the vinegar, chives and/or basil, salt and pepper. Serve at room temperature. Serves 3 to 6.

Fresh Ginger

Not so very long ago, it was almost impossible to find fresh ginger outside of Oriental grocery stores. Now it's everywhere, thank goodness, although I'm about the only person I know who buys it. It turns up in the cooking of all the Asiatic countries and also in the Caribbean, and adds a delightful tang to all sorts of dishes. Just add a minced tablespoon or so of it to soups, stews, stir-fries and even cakes.

Pick out the shiniest, freshest-looking ginger. The easiest way to handle it is: Using a half-pound or so at a time, wash and dry the ginger thoroughly. Cut into 1-inch pieces and run in a food processor or blender until it's very finely minced. Put into a jar. Add enough sherry or dry vermouth to cover. Keep refrigerated for last-minute, no-preparation use.

Growing your own ginger is theoretically possible if you live in a warm climate, but it's fussy and difficult work. Since it's now so widely available, you're better off buying it.

Teriyaki Sauce

Great to have on hand--and infinitely better than any you can buy in a bottle. Use it to marinate and/or baste anything you're planning to grill or broil--chicken, fish, hamburgers, vegetables, etc. Also for a deliciously authentic Oriental taste, add a tablespoon or two to any stir-fry.

1 teaspoon minced fresh ginger
1 teaspoon minced fresh garlic
2 teaspoons honey
1 tablespoon dry sherry
1 cup tamari or other soy sauce

Combine all the ingredients and keep refrigerated.

Real Gingerbread

The best gingerbread you've ever tasted. Gingerbread made with powdered ginger is certainly pale compared to this, the real thing.

1/2 cup butter
1/2 cup water
1/2 cup brown or raw sugar
1/4 cup unsulphured molasses
1/4 cup corn syrup or honey
1 egg
3 tablespoons finely minced or grated fresh ginger
    (the ginger in sherry mentioned previously is fine)
1 teaspoon baking soda
1 1/2 cups unbleached flour
1 cup raisins (optional)

Melt the butter in the water carefully, not letting it boil, in a large saucepan (which will also be your mixing bowl). Turn off the heat, stir in the sugar, molasses and corn syrup, then the egg and ginger. Combine the baking soda, flour and raisins, if you're using them, and beat this into the liquid mixture.

Bake in a well-greased 8-inch baking pan at 350° F. for about 35 minutes or until the gingerbread has shrunk a little from the sides of the pan. Frost with a butter icing or sprinkle with powdered sugar, if you want, but this gingerbread is good enough to be served just as it is.

Jicama

Jicama (pronounced <u>hee</u>-kah-mah) is a root vegetable with a light tan skin. In shape, it's like a turnip but much larger. In taste and texture, it's faintly like a crisp apple.

In Mexico, *jicama* is often eaten as a finger food, sliced and sprinkled with salt, chili powder and lime juice. Slices or wedges of *jicama* are an excellent addition to the usual carrot sticks, etc. you might serve with a dip, and it's refreshing in a salad. Cooked in a stir-fry, it will stay crisp.

Jicama seeds are available from Nichols Garden Nursery (see p. 32). While it can be grown anywhere, it takes 150 to 180 days to mature, so unless you live in the South, you may have to start your plants indoors.

Ensalada Esmeralda

Ensalada Esmeralda, Emerald Salad, is a delight. If you want to add rubies to it, sprinkle some pomegranate seeds on top.

1/2 cup peeled and diced *jicama*
1 avocado, peeled and diced
1 small zucchini, parboiled for 5 minutes, then sliced
2 peeled green chilies, diced
3 scallions, chopped
1 3-ounce package cream cheese, diced
1/4 cup cooked green beans or peas (optional)
oil and vinegar dressing
shredded romaine

Mix all the ingredients except the romaine together, tossing carefully so you don't break them up. Keep chilled. Serve on a bed of romaine. Serves 3 to 4.

Lemon Grass

Lemon grass, which looks like large chives, is one of the mainstays of Thai and other Southeast Asian cooking, and is now becoming popular in this country as well for the aromatic lemon peel-like flavor it adds to any food.

One simple way to use lemon grass is to bruise a stalk of it and cook it right along with, for instance, chicken broth or rice.

Whole lemon grass stalks, complete with their bulbs, are often available in Oriental grocery stores and large supermarkets. They'll keep for a least a week or two if you stand them in a glass of water.

To grow, find grocery store bulbs which bear wisps of root. Plant them in a sunny spot in the late spring. By the end of summer, you should have a good crop. If you live in a cold climate, transplant to pots in the fall and bring indoors.

Lemon Grass-Coconut Rice

Beautiful as a side dish or to serve with a simple curry.

2 cups grated unsweetened coconut (fresh, frozen or dried–
    look for it in Oriental groceries or healthfood stores)
2 cups boiling water
1 stalk lemon grass, bruised, then minced
1 cup rice

Put the grated coconut in a food processor or blender. Add the boiling water and run the machine for a full minute. Let the mixture sit until cool, then press through a fine strainer or a cheesecloth-lined colander.

Combine 1 1/2 cups of this coconut milk with the other ingredients in a medium-sized saucepan. Stir over medium- high heat until it comes to a full boil, then turn the heat down to the lowest possible setting, cover the pot and simmer for 25 minutes. Remove from the heat and let sit, covered, for 5 minutes. Serves 3 to 4.

Unusual Mushrooms

In one supermarket on the West Coast, I recently saw 12 different sorts of mushrooms, fresh and dry. While this is extreme, and most markets will probably never carry that many, there are still quite a few varieties in many stores these days --and most people keep right on buying the same mushrooms their grandparents did. Here are a few of the more popular of the new-to-the-market mushrooms, most of which, as you can tell by their names, have come to us from the Orient.

Spores for growing mushrooms of these sorts are not available for home production.

Enoki **mushrooms.** Imagine a bean sprout which is stretched straight out and you'll have some idea of what an *enoki* mushroom looks like. They're usually used raw--or, at most, cooked very briefly at the end of stir-frying or dropped into a hot broth just before it is served.

Osaka Salad

3 cups of tender greens--soft leaf lettuce (red as well as
      green), a little watercress, a bit of *arugula* and/or
      radicchio, perhaps some Belgian endive, etc.--
      torn into medium-sized pieces
1/2 cup *enoki* mushrooms, ends trimmed off
Japanese rice wine vinegar

Arrange the tender greens as decoratively as you can on four salad plates, then delicately and strategically place the mushrooms on top. Now drizzle on a bit of rice wine vinegar and serve at once. Serves 4.

Shiitake mushrooms. Chinese black mushrooms. Cloud Ears. These three mushrooms are, if dried (as they usually are), treated in the same fashion: Soak in very hot water for 30 minutes or more, until soft, then cut off and discard stems. (In the case of cloud ears, cut off and discard the woody parts.) Use the sliced tops of either fresh or dried *shiitakes* in any salad or stir-fry. Use Chinese black mushrooms and cloud ears in such Chinese specialties as:

Hot and Sour Soup

4 cups chicken broth
4 Chinese black mushrooms, soaked and trimmed
1 cloud ear, soaked (separately) and trimmed
1 small can bamboo shoots
1 small pork chop, boned
1 cake of tofu (fresh bean curd), which can be found in
      most supermarkets, usually in the produce section
3 tablespoons red wine vinegar
2 tablespoons light soy sauce
1/2 teaspoon freshly ground black pepper
1/2 teaspoon salt
2 tablespoons cornstarch, dissolved in 2 tablespoons water
2 eggs, beaten
1 1/2 tablespoons Oriental sesame oil
Oriental hot oil

Bring the chicken broth to a boil in a large pot. Cut the mushrooms, bamboo shoots, pork chop and tofu into matchsticks. Add to the broth along with the vinegar, soy sauce, pepper and salt. Boil gently for 2 or 3 minutes, then give the cornstarch mixture a stir and add it to the pot. Stir until the soup has thickened. Remove the pot from the heat and stir in first the eggs, then the sesame oil, then 3 or 4 drops (or more, depending on your taste) of hot oil. Serves 4 to 6.

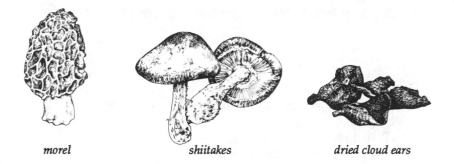

morel   shiitakes   dried cloud ears

Morels. (Pronounced as in the word morals.) These are considered a major delicacy in French cooking, but their high price puts them out of reach for the average cook, and under lock and key by many produce managers. Your best bet is to go out in the woods and find your own--after first consulting a reliable guide to wild mushrooms.

Creamed Morels

Creamed morels call for candlelight, champagne and an exceedingly well-padded bank account (unless you find your own morels).

1 pound fresh morels, cleaned and trimmed
2 tablespoons butter
1 tablespoon olive oil
1 tablespoon flour
1 cup heavy cream
1 tablespoon Madeira

Sauté the morels in the butter and olive oil over medium-low heat for 10 minutes, or until lightly browned. Now mix in the flour and stir for about 2 minutes before adding the cream and Madeira. Cover and simmer over very low heat for 10 minutes. Serve on toast to 4 plutocrats.

Plantains

Plantains, although a fruit, are included because they are always treated like a vegetable and because, in addition to being new to most markets and unfamiliar to most cooks, they are so very good.

Plantains look like large bananas, but are different in one major way: They have to be cooked before they are eaten. These Caribbean fruits are a bit tricky to peel. Use a small sharp knife to make slits down the ribs of the plantain. The skin will then come off easily.

Plantain chips or the thicker version known as *tostones* are make the nicest appetizer you could imagine and can also be served as a vegetable. Very ripe plantain slices or chunks can be cooked in any sort of soup or stew.

Plantains can only be grown in tropical climates.

Tostones

green plantains
oil for shallow frying
salt

Peel plantains, then slice diagonally 1/2 inch thick. Cook in about 2 tablespoons of oil in a frying pan over medium-high heat until tender but not brown, adding more oil if needed. Drain on paper towels, then smash each *tostone* down to about half its former height. You can do this with your hands or between two sheets of waxed paper.

When you're almost ready to serve, re-cook the *tostones* in the oil until brown and crisp on both sides. Drain on paper towels, sprinkle with salt and serve hot.

One plantain will make 12 to 15 *tostones*, which will serve 2 people.

Plantain Chips

green plantains
oil for deep-fat frying
salt

Peel the plantains, then slice them as thin as you can with the thinnest slicing blade of a food processor, for instance. Let them sit in cold water for about 20 minutes, then dry well.

Fry in deep fat at about 375° F. until they look like potato chips. Drain, then sprinkle with salt. Count on the chips from one plantain for each two people to be served.

Calypso Chicken

1 frying chicken, cut into quarters (or an equivalent
   amount of chicken parts)
2 tablespoons oil
1 1/2 cups chopped onion
1 teaspoon minced fresh garlic
1 very ripe plantain (the skin should be black),
   cut into 3/4-inch slices
3/4 cup chicken broth
3 cups diced tomatoes
1/4 cup chopped *cilantro* or flat-leaved parsley
1 teaspoon ground cumin
1/2 teaspoon Louisiana hot sauce (but only 1/4 teaspoon
   if using Tabasco sauce, which is ultra-hot)

Fry the chicken pieces, onion, garlic and plantain slices in the oil. When the chicken is brown on both sides, pour off the excess oil and add all the remaining ingredients. Simmer, covered, for 30 minutes. Serve hot (but it can be made ahead and reheated) on rice. Serves 4.

Radicchio

Radicchio (pronounced rah-<u>dee</u>-kee-oh) is one of the most amazing-looking things to turn up in produce departments in the last few years. Look for what resembles a small (fist-sized), elongated, tightly bunched head of lettuce--but instead of green, it will be red and white. (I recently saw it in a small store with a label saying, "Red Boston Lettuce.")

In this country *radicchio* is generally added to salads for a touch of color and sharpness of flavor. In Italy, its home, it is more often treated as a vegetable, grilled or braised as you would Belgian endive, which it resembles in taste.

Radicchio is expensive in stores, but simple to grow. Seeds are widely available and the culture is the same as for lettuce.

Grilled Radicchio

4 heads *radicchio*
2 tablespoons olive oil
salt and freshly ground black pepper to taste

Split the *radicchio* lengthwise. Cook over a hot charcoal fire, basting with the olive oil, sprinkling with the salt and pepper and turning the halves a time or two until they're light brown.

To cook indoors, heat the olive oil in a frying pan over medium-high heat. Pan-broil the *radicchio* halves in this, sprinkling with the salt and pepper and turning them until they're light brown. Serves 4 to 8.

Braised Radicchio

4 heads *radicchio*, split in half lengthwise
2 tablespoons butter
1/4 cup chicken broth
the juice of 1/2 lemon
just a little freshly ground pepper

Melt the butter in a large frying pan over low heat. Add the *radicchio* halves and cook gently for 2 or 3 minutes, turning often. Add the rest of the ingredients, cover tightly and simmer very slowly for about 35 minutes, or until extremely soft. Serves 4 to 8.

Rapini

Rapini has many aliases: Bitter broccoli, broccoli raab (its name in some seed catalogs), broccoli rabe, cime di rape and even just rape. The produce departments seem to be settling down to *rapini*. It's a non-bunching broccoli, a leafy green sometimes topped with small yellow flowers.

Whatever the name, you can cook it alone or with other greens or eat tender shoots raw (in a salad, for instance).

Seed is available from a number of companies. Sow directly in the ground in late spring.

Rapini with Pine Nuts

In this recipe, the bitterness of the *rapini* is toned down by adding spinach. If you don't find this necessary, just use an extra pound of *rapini* instead of the spinach.

1 bunch (about 3/4 pound) *rapini*
1 pound spinach
1/4 cup olive oil
2 teaspoons minced garlic
1/4 cup pine nuts
2 tablespoons red wine vinegar
salt and freshly ground black pepper to taste

Trim and thoroughly wash both the *rapini* and spinach. Boil the *rapini* in a large quantity of salted water for 10 minutes or until tender. Drain. Cook the spinach, covered, in just the water that clings to its leaves, for 6 minutes or until tender. Drain. Combine the two greens and chop somewhat coarsely.

Heat the olive oil in a large frying pan or wok over medium heat. Add the garlic and pine nuts and cook until they just begin to brown, then stir in the greens and stir-fry for 3 or 4 minutes more. Just before serving, stir in the red wine vinegar and season to taste with salt and pepper. Serves 4.

Squash Blossoms

Squash blossoms, often with tiny yellow or green squash attached, are frequently available in summer, either in markets or your own garden. If you have the usual too-much- zucchini problem, eating the blossoms will certainly take care of it! Pumpkin blossoms can be used in the same manner.

Crisp-Fried Squash Blossoms
With Mustard Sauce

A great appetizer, especially with the mustard sauce below, as well as a lovely vegetable dish.

15 squash blossoms
2/3 cup flour
1/2 cup water
vegetable oil for frying
salt

Rinse the blossoms gently, dry well and cut in half lengthwise. If tiny squashes are attached, cut them in half, too. Make a batter by stirring the flour slowly, bit by bit, into the water. Heat about 1/2 inch vegetable oil in a frying pan or wok until very hot (about 375° F.) Coat a few blossoms at a time with batter and cook in the oil, browning first one side, then the other. Drain on paper towels and sprinkle with salt. Makes 30 very crisp little blossoms, which can be reheated in an oven.

Mustard Sauce:
1 tablespoon dry mustard
3/4 cup sugar

1/2 cup cider vinegar
3 tablespoons water
2 beaten eggs

Combine the mustard and sugar in a saucepan, then stir in first the vinegar and water, then the eggs. Stir over medium heat until the sauce boils and thickens. Will keep indefinitely under refrigeration and can be reheated.

Tomatillos

The *tomatillo*, a gift from Mexico, has a husk-like outer skin and doesn't look particularly edible. It happens to be delicious, though, and those who like Mexican cooking have been buying *tomatillos* in cans for years. As with most things, fresh is better, and they're now available in many produce departments--or you can grow your own. They taste a bit like regular green tomatoes, but have a character all their own.

To use, remove the papery husk, then wash and dry. Your *tomatillos* are now ready to be cooked whole or chopped up and cooked in any sort of stew (chili, for example). They can also be ground to make a superb *salsa* for use as a relish or to top tacos and enchiladas or even broiled chicken or fish.

Tomatillos can be grown from seed. But be careful; there are similar-sounding vegetables in many cata- logs. What you want is *physalis ixocarpa*. (See Burpee's, p. 32.)

Salsa de Tomatillo

You can use raw *tomatillos* for this sauce. Some, however, prefer to cook them first, by simmering gently in water to cover for 20 minutes, stirring carefully a time or two.

1/2 pound *tomatillos*, husked, rinsed and cut in half
2 serrano chilies, canned or fresh (or substitute canned
    peeled green chiles plus a dash or two of hot sauce)
1/2 teaspoon minced or crushed fresh garlic
3 tablespoons minced onion
4 sprigs *cilantro*, chopped
a dash each of salt and sugar (both are optional,
    but do help to bring out the flavor)

Run all the ingredients together in a blender or food processor, adding just a little water, if needed. For a typical Mexican *salsa*, stop processing when there's still a lot of texture, before it becomes a smooth sauce. Makes about 1 1/2 cups.

Fresh Water Chestnuts

Fresh water chestnuts, which taste entirely different from the canned variety, look the way you'd imagine freshly-dug truffles would--small, dark brown and earthy. It's a nuisance to peel off the brown skin, but well worth the trouble. To use, rinse well, peel, rinse again, then eat raw or in a stir-fry. Or scrub, boil for 15 minutes, then peel and slice and serve either buttered or plain or in a salad. Use them whenever water chestnuts are called for in a recipe. Keep peeled water chestnuts covered with water and refrigerated until you're ready to use them.

If all you've ever tried are canned water chestnuts, the sweetness and lack of canned taste will be a happy revelation. Sorry, but you can't grow them at home (unless you have an Oriental mud paddy handy).

Water Chestnuts with Snow Peas

3 tablespoons oil
1/2 pound fresh water chestnuts, peeled and
     coarsely chopped
1/2 pound snow peas, trimmed, with any strings removed
1 tablespoon dry sherry
salt to taste

Heat oil over medium-high heat to about 375° F. Add the water chestnuts and snow peas and stir-fry for about 1 minute. Add the sherry and salt. Cook for another 30 seconds. Serves 4.

Seed Sources for Gourmet Vegetables

W. Atlee Burpee & Company
(available in many garden shops)
300 Park Avenue
Warminster, PA 18991

Fredonia Seeds
(available in many supermarkets)
Fredonia, NY 14063

Harris Seeds
961 Lyell Avenue
Rochester, NY 14606

Park Seed Company
Cokesbury Road
Greenwood, SC 29647-0001

Johnny's Selected Seeds
Foss Hill Road
Albion, ME 04910

Nichols Garden Nursery
1190 North Pacific Highway
Albany, OR 97321